SHEEBA VA

CONFIDENCE
CLARITY & EASE

A GUIDE FOR EMERGING LEADERS TO THRIVE

Title: Confidence, Clarity & Ease - A Guide For Emerging Leaders To Thrive.

By Sheeba Varghese

ISBN: 978 1 7354342 0 9

TO GET IN TOUCH:

Email: sheeba@coachsheeba.com

Phone: USA +1 650 - 741 - 6545

Website: www.coachsheeba.com

TABLE OF CONTENTS

ACKNOWLEDGEMENTS

I want to thank my husband, Santosh, for his encouragement to get this book started. Thank you, JoAnn, for your gentle nudge when I didn't feel that this was possible. Thank you, Wambui, for your patience with me on this process.

I want to thank my sons, Samuel and Steven - it is because of you that I have learned so much of what leadership means. I thank my family for always encouraging me to step outside of my comfort zone; Jason, thank you for helping me to get clarity on the title for this book.

I want to thank all those who have been telling me for years to write! I want to thank all the leaders out there who I have worked with one-on-one and in group settings. Our work together has been the catalyst to write this guide.

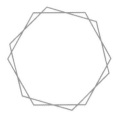

FOREWORD

"A leader is one who knows the way, goes the way and shows the way."
~ John C. Maxwell

I have known Sheeba for a couple of years now and one of the things she is a natural at, is the lifestyle of leadership. I wouldn't let that single word fool you, "Leadership". It is a weighty word. I have observed that it is not the topic of leadership that often feels theoretically static and even stagnant. Leadership is a lifestyle, full of fluid movement, foresight and is constantly evolving in so many ways. It is not a position or a title, it becomes you. Sheeba has with much grace become the essence of leadership, even as she has imparted it to those whom she coaches.

She is more keen to shed light on the issue and solve the problem, and not so much fix you. She digs out issues with delicate and profound questions that cause you to look deeper within. When the light is shone on what needs to change, she will hold your hand and walk you through it. She will elevate your thinking and amplify the strengths and good already going on with you. Sometimes you already have it, but you either play it down or have been blinded by circumstances or situations that are not of your own doing. This is when you need a 'Sheeba' to see it and put emphasis on it till you can see it too. Only you can want the change, only you would recognize when the change is happening. Her part is to guide you, to urge you on and most importantly, to act as a catalyst both in the overall bigger picture and more so in the detail of your journey.

She is coaching and calling you forward into your own life, even when she is not aware that she is doing it. This is because sometimes it is wrapped in relationship and friendship as is the case for me. I have had the privilege of receiving her as a catalyst in certain areas of my life. I am still in the process of receiving from her as I desire to grow in the area of leadership. In life, my motto has always been to remain teachable. As a result of this, I am constantly evolving with pretty much every conversation I have with Sheeba. It may be in easy banter or an actual resolution of a personal issue. I have enjoyed her candor, as well as the results that come from her skillful guidance.

This book is exactly that. Guidance, whether alone in the privacy of your home or an introduction to what could be for you. I hope it opens you up to the more that could be for you. Be it embracing and being curious about leadership or reaching out to Sheeba in one of her courses. Receiving her, and receiving from her has been a treasure for me.

Wambui Ngabura

ARTIST & INDUSTRIAL DESIGNER.

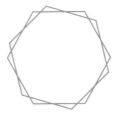

INTRODUCTION

Recently, I read that the top three sources that leaders chose as having shaped their leadership development experience came from; their work experience, being a parent/guardian and time spent in management positions. I found that interesting because although I have never worked *in* Corporate America, I have closely interacted with those who have and are still working in Corporate America. I have worked with those in small businesses and large ones. I have worked in schools with young people and most importantly, I have worked at home in training our sons along with my husband. I have to say that much of what I have learned about leadership has come from my time teaching in high school and raising my sons.

We often look at a special group of people as leaders, but leadership is not reserved only for people in management positions. Every day you affect those around you. Every day, you lead - whether you realize it or not, because leadership applies to both personal and professional situations. The question really is about how well you are leading in your spheres. It doesn't matter if you run a Fortune 500 company, work within the different levels of the corporate ladder, have a family, are involved in a relationship, or volunteer within your communities, we all need to improve our leadership skills because it will impact the sphere we are called to influence. Some are called to greater measures of influence than others, but all of us have a measure that we are responsible for and the key is to identify the sphere of influence you are called to impact. Remember, you do have an impact on those around you whether you realize it or not. This is what leadership is about. Your impact can transform the lives around you or it can drive people away. What is the impact you would like to have?

Regardless of the title, position, the company or business, the patterns that I have observed over the years are similar; they are often centered around identity, relationships, and processes. Some of these are, fears of not being good enough or not valued enough, effective strategies on how to lead others, feeling burnt out, overwhelmed by the amount of work, frustrations around giving feedback, communicating effectively, dealing with different personalities, managing conflict, and most recently the challenges around remote leadership. Does any of this resonate for you? Well, how different is this in our personal lives? It truly isn't. We just try to compartmentalize our lives and in essence how we show up in one place is how we show up in other places too.

Are you exhausted, overwhelmed by your team, or tired of trying to meet the expectations of your boss? Perhaps, you were just promoted into a position that you really did not want, or there is a position you really want and your leadership is hinting that you need to make some changes.

Do you have someone on your team that you have identified as a real challenge?

Are you trying to do things differently, trying to make some changes, but still feeling like it is not good enough? Are you managing someone either much younger or much older than you, and not sure how to be as effective as possible? Does your boss' expectations of you feel unrealistic? Does it feel like there is just not enough time in the day to do all that you need to do without feeling spent?

This book is in response to these types of concerns and others that I have heard from many of the leaders and teams that I have coached, mentored, and trained in one shape or another. You may resonate with some more than others. I do want you to know that you are not alone in feeling the way you do and that you don't have to remain in that state.

Utilize this resource as an invitation for you to consider how you might bring more levels of consideration and change to yourself, your relationships that are within your spheres, and within your practical leadership skills. My desire for you is that you will manage and lead others with confidence, clarity and ease.

ARE YOU PRODUCTIVE OR BUSY?

"It's not always that we need to do more, but rather that we need to focus on less."
~ Nathan W. Morris

There are so many things being thrown at you on a daily basis - whether it is from your boss, your direct reports, or your customers. In the world of remote work, it can seem as if you are going from one conference call to the next without a break in between. You are putting in those longer hours, trying to push out deadlines while juggling more responsibilities.

To make matters worse, you might often reach the end of a busy day and still feel like you have not been productive. In your mind you are asking yourself, "What did I actually do today?" It may feel like you are putting out fires or spinning your wheels, but not really moving forward or making real progress.

"What did I actually do today?" I have heard one too many leaders ask that question of themselves. And like I have done with many of my clients, I would turn that question back to you, "What did you actually do today?" Where did your time go? Time is here to serve you, but it seems like time is controlling you.

You give of yourself and feel like you can do it all until you quickly learn that you cannot. You forget to honor your time by disregarding your wellness, your family, your personal time or what you were actually hired to do. You might even have that open-door policy where anyone can interrupt you at all hours of the day. It could be an actual door that is open or the constant ping on a chat channel, which then leads to numerous interruptions throughout your day. Although, this can provide some immediate relief, over time these behaviors are not sustainable solutions for you or your team.

I call this the "busy but not productive" syndrome.
What has been the cost of working this way?
As you look at the list below, which statements ring true for you?

The cost has been

| I feel burnt out. |
| I feel like I am always playing catch up. |
| I feel disorganized. |
| I have not had a chance to look at long term goals. |
| I feel like I am putting out fires. |
| I am not getting my own work done. |
| My team is feeling stressed. |
| When I continue to do everything, my team is not being developed. |

What other cost would you add to the list above?

_____

_____

Why do we engage our day like this?

Sometimes, we do this because we want to be seen as a valuable person, as a team player and this driving force comes with a heavy price tag. Eventually, we lose focus and sight of what needs to be done because there are too many competing priorities vying for our time, anchored by the reality that it is difficult for us to say "NO!".

Other times, we keep busy because we are daunted by the task or project we should be focusing on. Thus, the overwhelm coupled with anxiety and fear propels us to do everything else but the very thing that requires our attention. Having watered this belief, the task or project falls further down our list and procrastination sets in. Sadly, the knowledge that it still needs to get done never goes away.

The reality may mean that the task or project cannot be finished during one session, but it may mean that it will need to be worked on over a couple of sessions scheduled throughout the week. Yet, there are personality types that do not like to start something if it cannot be finished in one sitting. How realistic is that? It isn't.

What we resist will persist! Do not allow busyness to distract you from what truly needs your attention.

Productivity is about completing actions that move you closer to accomplishing your goals in a manner that brings harmony and ease to your life. It is not enough to just mark tasks off a list. The tasks you are completing need to be directly related to achieving meaningful objectives. It is important to learn how to work more efficiently, so that you can have enough time to focus on your immediate responsibilities, your short-term goals and the future goals of your team, business, or company.

What does productivity require from you?

1. It requires you to prioritize your responsibilities. Take the time to do this. This may involve conversations with your team and your manager to clarify the priorities. You may have to do this every 4-6 weeks, just so everyone is on the same page. Regardless of the frequency, take time to do this.

2. It requires you to say "NO". Many times, we don't say no when we need to, because we feel it will be perceived a certain way. However, when you continue to say "yes" to everything, you will create an environment for yourself and your team that will not be sustainable over time.

3. It requires you to ask for help. This means that you will have the opportunity to delegate to others on your team. Delegation is important so others can

grow in their career trajectory. The challenge with delegation is trusting the person we want to delegate a task or project to before we delegate to them. That is totally understandable, and trust and delegation goes hand in hand. You cannot delegate a task or project and, like a crock pot, set it and leave it. You have to ensure there are scheduled times for check-in's, so progress, delays, questions, and challenges can be addressed.

Projects or tasks that I need to prioritize:

Questions for you to reflect on:

- As you consider your day, on a scale of 1 to 10 (10 being productive), how productive are you?

  _____

  _____

  _____

- What keeps you in a space of busyness?

  _____

  _____

  _____

- What must you do to identify your priorities?

  _____

  _____

  _____

- What support can you put in place to better manage the distractions that might come your way?

  _____

  _____

  _____

How can you become more productive?

1. Schedule time with yourself. This is half the battle, but it is important to block off a minimum of three hours a week on your calendar that you can call anything you desire. If three hours feels too much or not feasible, then begin with one hour. However, be intentional to block this time off on your calendar. Name this time as: Admin Time or Me Time. What matters most is that you actually do it. Small steps lead to sustainable habits over time.

2. Turn off all technological devices that could distract you during this specified time.

3. Use this time to catch up on work that has been sitting around for a while. Do not worry if you can't finish it up during that time. The idea is to begin it and continue to work through it.

4. Take time to answer the following questions:

What are you ignoring right now that really needs your attention? You need to schedule time to do this.

_____

_____

_____

What is something on your schedule right now that someone else can probably do better than you or should be trained to do? This probably needs to be delegated.

_____

_____

_____

What is something on your schedule right now that is a total waste of your time and energy? This is something you need to minimize doing.

_____

_____

_____

Notes

_____

_____

_____

_____

_____

_____

_____

_____

_____

_____

_____

_____

_____

_____

_____

_____

_____

_____

You choose how you spend your time every day; allow it to serve you rather than have it as an excuse to delay your attention on the important things in your life.

UNIQUENESS

"Don't be a pigeon if you were born to be an eagle. Experience God's altitude for your life."
~ Dr. Myles Munroe

My husband and I have two sons, Samuel and Steven, and they are so different from each other. Yet, I have been in so many conversations where people continue to compare them. Samuel can never be Steven and Steven can never be Samuel. They are unique and what they offer and contribute in the world will look so different.

You are unique. Yet, how long have you spent your time comparing yourself to someone else? I have heard so many leaders wanting to be like so-and-so. How can you express the uniqueness that you bring while you compare yourself to another? Your time and energy are wasted on how you feel you should be, could be and really, are not.

In 2010 and onwards, I facilitated coach training programs. In the midst of those week-long intensives, I would model coaching to the participants. At the end, I would often hear, "Sheeba, I want to coach like you." To this I would respond, "I want you to coach like you."

You are truly a unique being. Among the billions of others who walk this planet, there is no one like you, and there will be no other (person) like you. You are unique, you are extraordinary, and you are here for a purpose. Remember, no one else can do what you do, quite like you! Yet, when all the unique pieces fit together as in a puzzle, or like threads woven within a tapestry, what begins to emerge is a beautiful picture. How does this connect within the workplace, business or organization? When individuals begin to understand their contribution and begin to collaborate with others without ego or self-interest, what you get is a well-oiled machine: people working together, being productive, and achieving results for everyone to enjoy.

Here are some elements of comparison I would like you to remember:

- Comparison only breeds competition.
- Your engagement in life will be enveloped by the competition.
- Your focus will be concentrated on what your competition is doing or not doing.
- Your wins will be celebrated from a vantage point of your competition's loss. Instead, the invitation that is available for you, is to encourage and acknowledge the uniqueness that you witness within one another.

Now, with that said, when you are around others that are different from yourself, it allows you to grow in the areas that do not necessarily come naturally to you. For example, with my two sons, Steven is quite outgoing and is a connector, while Samuel is reserved and has a short list of loyal friends. One flies by the seat of his pants and the other has everything planned out. Is there anything right or wrong with either approach? No, but they can both learn from each other, because different situations and people we meet, may require them to display different skills and attributes. So, Samuel learns that it is fine to do something spontaneously from his brother and Steven learns that planning is of great value and benefit for his life.

What am I saying? Although we are unique, being with others that are different from us allows us to get out of our comfort zones. The purpose then is to grow and mature in your leadership, not to compete.

Questions for you to reflect on:

- What are you comparing right now in your life, business, and/or family?

  _____

  _____

  _____

- Who are you comparing it to?

  _____

  _____

  _____

- What is happening as a result?

  _____

  _____

  _____

- What is one step you can take to change it?

  _____

  _____

How can you continue to cultivate the uniqueness that you bring to leadership?

1. When you find yourself comparing yourself to someone else, take a moment and be aware of the fact that you are doing it.

2. Ask yourself,

   ☐ "What is it exactly that I am comparing?"
   Is it a skill (i.e. speaking abilities, leadership abilities, writing, etc)?

   ☐ Is it a character trait that you are wanting more of in the way you lead others (i.e. patience, boldness, etc.)?

☐   Is it a process within a team or business that you feel you should try?

3. Work with a mentor, coach, consultant, or someone that you trust. Who is that for you?

_____

_____

4. Share whatever it might be that you feel you want to improve, do differently or try for the first time. These authentic conversations can shift to the motivations of why you feel that you fall short, want to improve, or try something for the first time.

What is your motivation?

_____

_____

_____

Is it to develop and grow or does it further your ego and desire for competition?

_____

_____

_____

5. Once you are aware of the motivation, identify (it could be one or all of them):

- The skill you might want to develop

_____

- The character trait you might want to practice

_____

- The processes you might want to try out within your current team or business

_____

Notes

Your gifts and talents will be uniquely expressed through you.

3

CAST A VISION

"Vision without a task is only a dream. A task without a vision is but drudgery.
But vision with a task is a dream fulfilled."
~ Anonymous

Covid -19 hit and businesses were scrambling to get a handle on how to pivot in order to respond to the changes that were happening in rapid succession, cadence and intensity. Overnight, leaders had to respond to how their employees were going to be supported through the pandemic. From identifying priorities, setting up new processes, to working closely with their teams in identifying the best platforms that would support remote work, leaders had to cast a vision that would help to maintain the progress through the months ahead. These kinds of situations and many others, are what is required of leaders on a daily basis; responses that require agility, awareness, and courage for the leader to forge ahead boldly.

Leadership requires you to bring the elevator up from the "grind" floor to having a higher perspective so you can cast a vision! Can you imagine being on a boat where the captain has no clue where he is headed? Well, that is how your team will feel being around you, if you do not cast a vision. The people you oversee will not know why they are doing the things they are doing; they will begin to lack motivation. They will not have a buy-in to the process. It almost begins to feel robotic after a while. Who wants to work for a leader like that? Would you? I know I definitely would not want to be in that type of culture.

At the "grind" floor, you are stuck in the weeds for prolonged periods of time, which then prevents you from paying attention to what is ahead. You lose sight of what changes might need to be made in personnel, processes and priorities, in response to the journey ahead. You can easily get caught in survival mode because the demands of your daily work, your deadlines, and your attention to what is right in front of you can keep you from seeing the bigger picture.

"Your elevation determines your horizon." - Sam Soleyn

Casting a vision means that you will have to pull yourself out of the day-to-day "grind" in order to reflect and get clarity on the vision. It means you must have a higher elevation that will provide for a different perspective. This requires discernment, agility, patience and the willingness to collaborate with others to steer the ship forward from a higher vantage point.

The reasons I may keep myself busy on the "grind floor" are:

1. _____
2. _____
3. _____

The impact of this to me:

1. _____
2. _____
3. _____

The impact to my team is:

1. _____
2. _____
3. _____

Questions for you to reflect on:

- Do you know what the vision of your team, company or business is?

  _____

  _____

- Does your team know the vision?

  _____

  _____

- When was the last time you reviewed it with your team?

  _____

  _____

How do you cast a vision?

1. Begin by answering the following questions:

- Where are you headed?

  _____

  _____

  _____

- Why are you going in that direction?

  _____

  _____

  _____

- How do those around you connect to that direction?

  _____

  _____

  _____

- What current changes in processes and personnel need to be made to support that vision?

_____

_____

_____

2. Share it with your team.

3. Identify those on your team that would be ideal to carry out the various elements of the vision.

Notes

_____

_____

_____

_____

_____

_____

_____

_____

_____

_____

_____

_____

_____

_____

_____

_____

_____

_____

Vision brings focus and clarity to the path that lies ahead. So, when the vision feels unclear, take time to step aside from all the noise and busyness to rest.

LEAD IN THE BENEFIT
OF THOSE UNDER YOUR CARE

"Leading for the benefit of others is a much more compelling and powerful motivation than leading merely to get ahead or to hit an arbitrary target."
~ Tony Dungy

Yes, the title for this chapter is a bit wordy. But read it again and take it slow. It is not just about helping your people or doing nice things for those around you. I am sure you have even heard people say, "Let's make this a win-win." Leading in the benefit of others is so much more than 'win-win'; it is a mindset with a view on caring, supporting and equipping those around you to thrive. Enveloped in this mindset is an attention towards cultivating relationships.

Leadership comes with responsibility. And you know that only too well - not only of the work that has to get done, but also of the people that are given to your care. When you lead in the benefit of others, it requires a shift in your mindset that addresses the motivation of WHY you do the things you do. What do I mean by that?

For example, your first question is not "What can you do for me?" instead you will shift to "What can I do for you?" When you make decisions, your question is not "How is this going to impact me?" instead you will shift to "How is this going to impact them?"

What do you see as the difference?

_____

_____

_____

Thus, the motivation of why you do the things you do, changes. You begin to create a culture that is selfless and unconditional. Let me tell you something - when this begins to happen, there is not a person that won't want to follow you because they see something totally different in you!

I have personally seen this happen with my husband time and time again, as he has advanced within the pharmaceutical companies. There have been many that have left money on the table to work with my husband. Why? For the simple reason, that he serves in the benefit of those under his care. How? He encourages them to put their families first. He looks for opportunities for those on his team to advance in their career. He gives them opportunities to step outside of their comfort zone and has often advocated for an employee's promotion and increase in pay. He is not threatened by those who want his job, those who might be more knowledgeable than him or those who receive the recognition. Instead, his desire is to see others thrive.

What happens when you lead in the benefit of those under your care?

- You suspend the notion of _"quid pro quo"_ – if you do something for me, I will do something for you.
- You take actions that are actually in the benefit of those that relate to you.
- You consider their needs first - wow, what a novel idea!
- You make a way for others to shine and grow beyond you.
- You are not intimidated by the brilliance you are surrounded by. Instead, you welcome it and make room for more.

Questions for you to reflect on:

- What are you doing to cultivate the relationships on your team?

  _____

  _____

  _____

- What do your employees need from you? Have you asked?

  _____

  _____

  _____

- What do you need from your employees? Have you shared it with them?

  _____

  _____

  _____

How do you lead in the benefit of those under your care?

1. Make time to meet with every individual on your team and be consistent.

2. Take time to develop and cultivate a relationship with them. It is not only important to find out how the various projects are going, but to also find out how they are doing in general (i.e. What are their hobbies? What are the fun things that they enjoy? What changes, if any, have they had to make in the last couple of months?). I have noticed that depending on the culture that leaders are from, some are quite adept at asking questions that go beyond work and others are not so comfortable with this.

3. Get to know their strengths and weaknesses. A bonus that I will share in this department is that our strengths when overused becomes our weakness (i.e. If you are loyal and you overuse this, you can become resigned).

4. Take time to understand the motivation behind what gets them up in the morning to come work with you.

5. Create an environment that supports their growth and career advancement. This cannot be done until you begin asking questions that allow you to see their values, their career aspirations, and the type of support they need to be successful.

Notes

_____

_____

_____

_____

_____

_____

_____

_____

_____

_____

_____

_____

_____

_____

_____

_____

_____

_____

_____

_____

_____

_____

*Make it your mission to create opportunities, connections, and learning for
those around you to develop and grow.*

IT IS TIME TO LISTEN

"If you plan to be a good leader at all... Listen fully, subjugate your arrogance and need to be "right", and your righteous indignation, for a few seconds.. because only then will you hear the whisper of truth."
~ *Tony Dovale*

It was Christmas 2019 and my sons were home, but I noticed a bit of tension between the two of them. Samuel, my oldest, had come home from University for his winter break and Steven now had his brother back home, in what he had relegated as his domain for the past several months. I was lying down on the couch and I could hear the constant bickering back and forth. I could feel the tension and I knew something was brewing. Little comments here and there and finally it broke open when a particular jacket was left on the couch. Samuel decided to wear Steven's jacket without asking him. In Samuel's eyes, it was no big deal. In Steven's eyes it was a big deal. Similarly, Steven got accepted into a college and told one of Samuel's best friend's brother before he even told his own brother. In Samuel's eyes it was a big deal. In Steven's eyes it was not a big deal.

Both situations were big deals.

They were both sharing something that they valued.

One valued loyalty and that he would know important information about his brother before others did. Samuel has his loyal friends and he wanted to be that loyal confidante to his brother. Yet, for Steven, everyone is viewed as his best friend.

The other valued the care of this special gift that was given to him unlike his other jackets. He interpreted Samuel's cavalier way of placing the jacket on the couch without putting it back as a disrespect to his things. To Samuel it was just another jacket but to Steven, it was what the jacket meant to him. Almost everything that Steven has carries a story of how it is special because of its connection or relation to a person, experience or time.

Take a pause. Silence your mind. Tune in and listen.

It was only after they could hear the story beyond the presenting drama, that they could truly hear and understand the heart of the matter. Until then, they were reacting and listening just to respond to each other and mainly to prove their own point.

Take time to pause from the overflowing words to prove your point.

Silence the conversations in your mind and get curious.

Take time to tune your ears to listen and to understand what is being said and not being said.

Although, this is hard to do in the heat of the moment or when we are excited to get our ideas across, the sooner we practice these three words (pause, silence, and listen), it will impact the ways in which we relate, communicate, and lead others. Developing the skills of listening is a continuous challenge and process.

What makes listening so important?

A focus on listening can lead to more effective teamwork, higher productivity, fewer errors, enhanced innovation and problem-solving, productive conflict, improved recruiting and retention, superior customer relations and more. As authors on leadership development have noted through the years, listening is not just a nice thing to do, it is essential and at the heart of everything we do!

There are several levels of listening that I have experienced and learned over the years. Included here are levels of listening from my years of experience with coaching that I have found extremely valuable and critical to every leader. People can listen for self, listen for information or listen for meaning. All three levels are valuable depending on the situation, the context, and the person we are speaking with. On average, we are often living at and comfortable with the first 2 levels: listening for self and listening for information. To engage in a deeper level of listening, it requires us to table our assumptions, our inner dialogue, and our desire to be right, so that we can truly listen and understand the meaning of what is being shared; this is what is required to develop those around us.

Levels of our listening

- Listening for self: This type of listening is all about listening for how the information concerns you. It brings the focus back on you. Think of a time when you were in the doctor's office. When the doctor is sharing some test results with you, the type of listening you are engaging in at that time is probably at this level. You are wondering how what is said will affect you.

- Listening for information: This type of listening is all about focusing on what is said. You might use this when you are in a webinar, a class, or in a meeting with your direct report. You might be listening at this level to respond by answering a question. In a conflict, you might be listening to respond with your point. If it is with your direct report or your spouse, this type of listening might have you respond so you can fix the problem.

- Listening for meaning: This type of listening delves deeper. You begin to hear more than the drama of what is being said. You notice the body language, the values, what is truly important to the person, and why it concerns them. In essence, you hear their heart. At this level, you are truly listening to understand the other person's point of view. You hear what is being said and what is not being said. Listening at this level requires you to get curious instead of thinking that you already know the answer.

Listening better will reward you with an entirely new level of communication and problem-solving skills. Robert Dittmer, in his book, 151 Quick Ideas to Improve Your People Skills, says that "the fundamental purpose of listening is to gather information about the other person, to understand where he's coming from, how she views a situation, or what he values. If you sit quietly and let others do the talking, you can have an excellent opportunity to learn, to gather information. And that can be very powerful—in several ways."

Questions for you to reflect on:

- What is the impact to you when you are not truly listening?

  _____

  _____

  _____

- What is the impact to your team when you are not truly listening?

  _____

  _____

  _____

- What practices do you need to put into place so that you are taking the time to hear the heart of the matter?

  _____

  _____

  _____

How can you improve your listening skills?

1. Remove distractions when you are speaking to someone. This sounds so easy and simple and yet, how many conversations have you had in the last week where you were interrupted by a text, a family member, an email, etc.

2. Table your assumptions, biases and judgements in favor of curiosity. Ask questions that will help you to get clarity and have understanding as to the heart of the situation.

3. Reflect what you have heard back to the person you are speaking with, to ensure that you are both on the same page (i.e. "What I have heard so far....").

4. In the midst of any conflict or challenge, take time to listen to the values that are not being honored. Listen for what the real concern is for the individual. If you don't know, ask the questions: "What is it that concerns you the most

out of this whole situation?" "What is really important to you?"

One step I will take to improve my listening is:

_____

_____

_____

The distractions that may arise in taking this step are?

_____

_____

_____

My motivation to take the step is:

_____

_____

_____

Notes

_____

_____

_____

_____

_____

_____

_____

_____

_____

_____

_____

_____

_____

_____

_____

_____

_____

_____

_____

If you are too busy talking, you will fail to hear the real concern - which is what informs you on whether you will need to provide advice, coaching, and/or training.

GIVING AND RECEIVING FEEDBACK

"It takes humility to seek feedback. It takes wisdom to understand it, analyze it and appropriately act on it."
-Stephen Covey

One of the courses I facilitate is called a "Group Mentor Coaching class" for the professional coaches who are looking to become credentialed with the International Coaching Federation. Many coaches often save this for last because this is a class in which they will be coaching in front of others, and will also be receiving feedback on their coaching. The very thought of this can be paralyzing for some, nerve-wracking for others, or just plain uncomfortable. As a facilitator, I endeavor to make this as painless as possible, because my hope is that the coaches walk away understanding that this process is not about assessment, but more about development. Isn't this how we all grow?

Giving AND receiving positive and constructive feedback is foundational to being an effective leader. This is not a one directional practice. Feedback goes both ways and it should not feel scary, but for many it is. Depending on the preferences and tendencies of our personality, feedback can feel like a personal attack. This viewpoint will never amount to anything fruitful.

Feedback is a gift, an opportunity to reflect and change how we communicate, relate, and/or lead others. It can be delivered in multiple ways. When done effectively, it will develop and motivate your team. Your team can be one person or many. It can be a classroom of students, your children, employees within a business, or a global team in an organization, to name a few.

What are some best strategies to employ when giving feedback?

1. Prior to giving any feedback, it is important to find out how the person likes to receive communication from you; this applies to both positive and constructive feedback. When you have taken this initiative even before you have to give feedback of any kind, you will have much more confidence when the time comes to share the feedback. Do not forget to share with your direct reports on how you would like to receive feedback, as well. This gives others the permission to share their thoughts with you too.

2. Before delivering the feedback, you will have to get clear with yourself as to what it is that you would like to give feedback about. What behaviors do you want to see more of/less of? What needs to stop because it will have an adverse effect? It may help to write it down and practice saying it out loud.

3. Avoid generalities and be specific as to what you observed, noticed or heard *("I observed...." "I noticed....and I am not sure if you are aware, but the impact of this to me/the team/a certain individual/the project was*

_____

_____ *"*).

   Be specific with your feedback, regardless of whether it is constructive or positive feedback. Employ words that will allow the person receiving the feedback to leave that conversation without any level of ambiguity.

4. Give opportunity for the person receiving the feedback to share their observations and what was going on for them (i.e. *"This is what I observed, but I always know that there are more sides to a story, so what was happening for you?"*).

5. Take the time to connect the feedback to the motivation around why it is being shared and the impact of the "said" behavior that you are discussing. When this is done for positive or constructive feedback, it allows the recipient to see more than just what he/she has done (i.e *"The reason I am*

sharing this is because your initiative galvanized the new members of the team to take action. I don't know if you know this, but you carry a lot of influence and it showed on this project. I want you to know how much of an influencer you are on this team.")

6. Take time to collaborate and/or discuss next steps. Sometimes you might have to be quite direct with your next steps and other times the discussion may lend to a more collaborative approach. This all depends on the context.

7. Schedule an appointment where you can come together to share how things are going; discuss what is working well and what is not.

So, for you leader, when was the last time you had a chance to take an inventory of yourself? How would you like to understand how you are showing up AND receive feedback, so you can become effective within your leadership sphere? This is a process I have completed with numerous leaders and it is called the '360 Assessment'. There are different tools and instruments you can use. However, at the heart of this exercise is that you identify about 7-12 individuals (those that report to you, those that are colleagues, your manager/boss, anyone else that you feel knows you pretty well or you even feel do not care much for you). This is something that you do when you are ready to really hear and recognize the patterns within the areas you are doing well in, the areas for growth and the areas for improvement. If you want to know more about this process or would like to have one completed for you, reach out to me and we can discuss this further.

The value of receiving feedback is best summarized by Jim Yong Kim, a physician and anthropologist who said, "No matter how good you think you are as a leader, my goodness, the people around you will have all kinds of ideas for how you can get better. So for me, the most fundamental thing about leadership is to have the humility to continue to get feedback and to try to get better – because your job is to try to help everybody else get better."

Questions to reflect on:

- When will you take the time to find out how your direct reports like to receive feedback?

  _____

  _____

  _____

- What is the mindset that you need to embrace so you do NOT receive feedback as a personal attack on you?

  _____

  _____

  _____

- How will you follow through when you receive or give feedback?

  _____

  _____

  _____

Notes

_____

_____

_____

_____

_____

_____

_____

_____

_____

_____

_____

_____

_____

_____

_____

_____

_____

_____

_____

_____

If you truly want to develop your leadership impact, you must ask the questions that will help you see how you are being perceived. This will inform you of the changes you might want to make.

7

DON'T GO AT IT ALONE

"A leader takes people where they want to go. A great leader takes people where they don't necessarily want to go, but ought to be."
~ Rosalynn Carter

I have had the beautiful opportunity to receive guidance, advice, coaching and counsel within my professional and personal life from a variety of mentors, coaches, and spiritual leaders. Each one has been special to me in the different stages and seasons of my life because it brought greater levels of clarity, direction, encouragement and comfort to me.

Over the years, I have come to realize that when you are going through the toughest times of your life, you do not need someone just to agree with you or soothe your emotions. You also need someone to help you see yourself as more than a victim of circumstance. You need someone to help you see beyond what is happening TO you….to what is happening for your benefit and growth.

These kinds of leaders have a vision for you and want you to come to a higher perspective. They help you to ask the question: "What am I learning through this?" as opposed to "Why is this happening to me?" This is a transition, a shift in our mindset that helps us to view life and all that we are going through from a different lens.

What else have I found true about these kinds of leaders?

- They have character and maturity.
- They are not defined by their titles or accolades, although they may often

have them.

- They are humble and willing to serve.
- Their success is seeing others successful - seeing others equipped in their full potential.
- What else might you add to this list?

_____

_____

_____

As the seasons in your personal and professional life change, recognize the need for such leaders. You were not called to walk this journey alone. We need one another.

We can attend classes, read books, listen to podcasts, but working one-on-one with a person gives you the opportunity to receive personalized support. It is my deep desire that you are able to connect to someone whose relationship can elevate your perspective and as a result expand your leadership influence.

Leaders that have impacted my life:	The impact to me was:

Questions to reflect on:

- When was the last time you had a chance to let down your guard, become vulnerable and truly speak with someone that you knew had your best interest at heart?

  _____

  _____

  _____

- What is the belief, fear, assumption, or concern that keeps you from being transparent with someone?

  _____

  _____

  _____

How might you work with a mentor?

1. Consider a person in your life that you can be totally transparent and vulnerable with both in good times and bad.

2. Be intentional to pursue this person and set times to meet with him/her.

3. No one can answer the questions that are not being asked. So, be purposeful in asking questions about areas in your life that you might be struggling with or concerned about. This is your opportunity to be transparent.

Notes

Inheritance in life is not simply money, but it is the wealth of wisdom that comes from those who have walked ahead of us and are able to share from their vault of experience for our benefit and growth.

RESPOND VS. REACT

"The possibilities are endless once we decide to act and not react."
~ George Bernard Shaw

When you are in a tough situation do you tend to respond or react? Both are applicable given the context we are given. However, living in a constant state of reacting to situations can get quite tiresome over time. It can affect our overall perception, our health and our ability to see or hear at a greater depth.

What is the difference?

When we react, it is often a knee-jerk, sudden blurting out of what is on our mind. We have not taken the time to consider or value the person beyond the issue. We have only looked at the situation in terms of how it might affect ourselves.

And when we respond? Well, this is where we have taken the time to consider other sides so that we can understand what might be best for the situation and people at hand.

What makes this so difficult for many? This takes a level of restraint over our emotions, and maturity to see beyond the immediacy of the situation. It requires us to become proactive in our approach. Although this can take time to achieve, it is a behavior that we can all practice.

Working with many leaders, I have found that it is easier for some personalities more than others. There are those personalities that have tendencies and preferences that attend life in such a manner that they consider others and the impact of a decision or task with greater levels of consideration, while others are much faster paced in life. What is your tendency? Fast-paced and at times impulsive or slower-paced and contemplative?

The answer to that question will inform you on the discipline that will be required of you: restraint to not react so quickly or not waiting too long to respond.

Questions to reflect on:

- Do you tend to respond or react in life?

People I find myself reacting to:

Types of situations that cause
me to be impulsive:

_____

_____

_____

_____

_____

_____

_____

Types of situations that cause me to
delay in my response:

_____

_____

_____

_____

_____

_____

_____

What is the belief or assumption that I am making that causes me to be impulsive or delay in my response?

How can you respond effectively in leadership?

1. When you are faced with decisions, challenges, drama and obstacles, learn to pause before you react or respond.

2. Before you shoot off a message in any type of technological platform, take time to revisit the way it was stated. Remember, the written word might not translate the same way as when spoken. Don't hit "send" right away.

3. If you have a tendency to be slow to respond, give yourself a deadline so you can reply in a timely fashion. You can also ask for a deadline for the response from the person requesting information.

4. When there are challenging situations that pull on you to emotionally react, speak with someone that can be objective with you. This is a great reason to work with a leadership coach, because within that type of engagement you have the freedom to share, voice your concerns and frustrations in a safe space. It is also within this space that your coach will ask questions that will bring about a greater level of awareness for you, in how you could and may want to respond.

Notes

_____

_____

_____

_____

_____

_____

_____

_____

_____

_____

_____

_____

_____

_____

_____

_____

_____

_____

_____

_____

What you say and how you respond will inevitably shine a light on your maturity and character.

TAKE TIME TO DEVELOP
THE PEOPLE AROUND YOU

"The growth and development of people is the highest calling of leadership."
~ Harvey S. Firestone

Yes/No	How true are these statements?
	I am purposeful in developing the people around me.
	I am not doing all the work myself because I have been effective in delegating the work to those around me.
	I know the strengths of those on my team.
	I know the limitations of those on my team.
	I know the "why" of those around me.
	I know the communication styles of those around me.
	I know the best way to give feedback to those around me.

It is your responsibility to support, develop, encourage, champion, and open doors for those around you to thrive. Sometimes, you will find that leaders do not do this.

Why?

- They are afraid of people leaving after all that time was invested in developing the individual.

- They fear someone might take their position.

- There is just not enough time in the day to do this.

Regardless of the reason, sometimes those fears become the motivation to do everything yourself or give just enough to those around you to make it work.

You cannot do everything. You are not supposed to do everything. Again, take the elevator up from the "grind" floor and if you want to become an exceptional leader, this mindset shift of adapting a coach-like approach to your leadership style is critical. Michael Bungay Stanier has a great book called, *The Coaching Habit: Say Less, Ask More & Change the Way You Lead Forever.* In this book, there is great effort taken to help leaders to facilitate conversations that allow for deeper levels of listening, powerful questioning followed by accountability. All of this is premised on the foundational principle that those around us are adults that are resourceful and capable of taking ownership and responsibility for the work that they are doing. If they always come to you for advice, then you will eventually fail to build them up to develop. If we always solve the problem, how do others learn to solve their own problems?

As I have spoken about the levels of listening before, I want to take a moment here to talk about the types of questioning, because each type has a different purpose and place in the context of leadership and specifically when we are developing others.

- Surface questions: The surface types of questions are those that we ask in our everyday conversations. These questions engage others at the surface level and the answers are just enough to keep a conversation going without any level of depth.

- Fixing questions: The questions in this realm lead YOU to fix the problem or challenge. While there is nothing wrong in asking these types of questions, over the long haul, you are seen as the "fixer". When you are viewed as the fixer, you may find yourself carrying unnecessary burdens, getting frustrated because people decide to do something totally different than what you suggested, or you find yourself getting burned out by the constant reliance on you.

- Equipping questions: I believe there are different degrees of equipping questions. From projects, goals or tasks to challenges, conflict or drama, equipping questions places the responsibility and ownership in the hands of the person or team you are asking the question to. On one hand, equipping questions can help individuals and teams become clearer on resources, time, and support that might be needed. While on the other hand, it can help to bring awareness to a person's relationship to their challenge, obstacle, drama, conflict, _____

  _____

(feel free to put your own word in there)

Equipping questions are not long-winded or leading. They are asked from a place of curiosity and a desire to develop others to grow in confidence and clarity. They encourage the person to gain greater levels of awareness and become equipped, so that when they are within the situation again with different actors or actresses, different companies or businesses, but with the same drama, similar goals or outcomes, they are able to confidently address the issue with clarity and ease.

All of these questions are valuable given the context and the person you are speaking with. Are you training someone? Are you developing someone to lead? Are you tasked with fixing a problem? Are you teaching?

Questions	Empowering Questions
• Did you complete the project?	• What has been completed?
• Do you have any questions?	• What went well?
• Is this clear?	• What did you find challenging?
	• What would you do differently?

Notice how quickly one can answer the questions in the first column with a simple yes or no. The second column is about equipping another to think deeply and to take ownership around their responsibilities.

Start to look around you and consider the ways you would go about developing the people around you. I will tell you now, this will require your time and intention to understand the people you are surrounded by and if you are working remotely, you will need to make an extra effort to be intentional about this. This does not happen overnight. But over time, you will begin to see ripple effects around you. It WILL create sustainable change.

Questions for you to reflect on:

• What comes in the way of you developing those around you?

_____

_____

_____

• What is one fear that you might have in developing those around you?

_____

_____

_____

- Look at the table on page 12. What statements were not true for you?

_____

_____

_____

How would you develop those around you?

1. Identify one person you would like to take the time to develop:

_____

_____

2. Acknowledge and have a conversation with them that will frame the conversation as to your intentions of what it is that you are hoping to create. Refrain from answering and fixing all the problems, challenges and questions that come your way. Instead, open the dialogue up and begin to ask equipping questions that allow and prepare your direct report to solve their own problems.

3. Take time to know the strengths, limitations, communication styles, motivation, and best ways to give feedback for every person on your team by simply asking the questions.

4. Remember to

Acknowledge who they are and what they have done

Provide opportunities that will allow them to grow beyond their comfort zone

Provide positive and constructive feedback

Delegate projects and tasks that will help them grow in their career

Notes

Developing others around you takes time and it requires a mindset in which
you begin to see others as resourceful and capable.

10

REMOTE LEADERSHIP

*"You can never over-communicate enough as a leader at a company, but at a
remote company, nothing could be truer."*
~ *Claire Lew*

In the wake of the COVID-19 pandemic, so many companies moved toward
working remotely. Over the years, we had seen companies transition to flex
teams, hybrid teams and now more than ever the emergence of fully remote
teams. Like teams in an office, there are common challenges that fully remote
teams experience as well: communication, cultivating relationships, managing
conflict, identifying the right platforms for virtual teams, creating clear priorities,
tracking performance and work/life balance to name a few.

Remote leadership requires you to be intentional, committed and focused on the
processes and the relationships within your sphere of influence.

There are four strategies to achieve this and these also work for teams that are
located in the office.

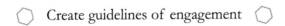 Create guidelines of engagement

Guidelines of engagement is a working document that you can create in collaboration with your team. It becomes a working document that everyone on the
team has given input to and has reached an agreement around what is stated.
Once that happens, it also becomes a source of holding one another accountable. I shared this idea with a teacher who decided to do this with her kindergar-
ten class. They came up with an agreement to how each student would behave in
her class and each student signed their name to the document.

Why are guidelines important?

- They give us a chance to understand how we are going to behave with one another.
- They help us understand what to do when problems arise.
- They encourage each person to take responsibility for their actions.
- They reinforce self-management and taking responsibility for personal growth, outcomes and goals.

Your next question might be: What is on the document?

The guidelines of engagement will address anything related to employees engaging one another and you.

Some of the behaviors you can address on this living document are:

1. Structure and schedule for meetings;
2. Acceptable behaviors during meetings—remember to talk about virtual meetings too;
3. Preferred method of communication (email, phone call, video chat, etc);
4. Timeline of responding to one another (especially important in global workforce);
5. Use of common resources - human and otherwise;
6. Availability of team members during non-work hours.

In order to address some of these behaviors listed above, here are some of the questions you can ask, discuss and have someone document:

- How do we ensure everyone will participate in a Video Conferencing meeting?
- What are the expectations during a virtual meeting?
- What is the communication response time when there is an email or call sent on Friday at the end of the work day?
- What other question(s) would you add to this list?

_____

_____

_____

- Who would benefit if you were to create guidelines of engagement with your team?

  _____

  _____

  _____

- What would be the cost of not setting this up?

  _____

  _____

  _____

How would you create the Guidelines of Engagement?

1. From the list above, what would you like to discuss?
2. Identify the questions you want to ask.
3. Call a team meeting, discuss the questions and come to an agreement.
4. Have a "scribe" type out the responses.
5. Get an agreement to hold people accountable.
6. Review them every 3-6 months to see what needs to be changed.

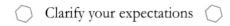

◯ Clarify your expectations ◯

On remote teams, communication can be harder, and setting clear expectations is so important as you are not able to see one another on a daily basis. Sherpa Executive Coaching program, has always shared with their executive clients that setting clear expectations is a valuable part of leadership. You must be clear to clarify expectations when something is not working, when something is new or when something has changed. You will notice the breakdown of systems and processes in a remote world much more quickly, than you would when people are working together in an office.

- What expectations do I need to clarify?

  _____

  _____

  _____

- Is there a brand new expectation that needs to be shared?
  Is there an expectation that has been changed and thus the changes need to be shared?

  _____

  _____

  _____

◯ Determine the right tools ⬡

There are so many tools that are available to companies and businesses out there. I would not presume to tell you what tool to use. Instead, what I would tell you, is that it is important to be consistent with the tool that you are going to use and to make sure everyone knows what tool is going to be used, and for what purpose. Take the guessing game out for your employees.

Determine the tools that would be used for:

- Document sharing and file storage
- Project Management
- Communication: Video, audio and collaboration
- Relationship building
- Time Management

What would you add to this list?

_____

_____

- What are the tools that you are using?

  _____

  _____

  _____

- What needs to be clarified to your team?

  _____

  _____

  _____

- And what tool will be used for what?

  _____

  _____

  _____

◯ Cultivate strong relationships ◯

Cultivating strong relationships becomes even harder when you are working remotely. Again, this takes special effort, time, and energy compared to before. I have worked with several leaders in this area that did not think this was important. Yet, once they experimented with several ideas, they could see the change in their teams.

So, what am I talking about? I am saying that it is important to have consistent meetings with your employees—have "town hall" gatherings so everyone can be on the same page—and then don't forget the part of doing something fun with your teams. I have had leaders who were not the greatest at organizing "fun stuff" with their teams and I have advised them to delegate that to those on their team that would love to do it. Again, you don't have to do everything yourself, however you do need to provide space for it to occur. You would not know who to delegate it to, unless you took the time to develop relationships with those around you.

Questions for you to reflect on:

- What gaps still exist as we work remotely?

  _____

  _____

  _____

- What needs to be fine-tuned?

  _____

  _____

  _____

Notes

_The level of intentionality in all areas of leadership must increase when we
are working remotely._

Some final thoughts

When I am coaching and training, I always encourage the participants to take one small step that would propel them forward in their development and growth. I will be doing the same as I come to the end of this book.

I see myself as a catalyst for change. In being a catalyst, I have always been one to see the potential in others. Although, I might be able to see it, it is you that has to realize it, actualize it, live into it and be it.

I do believe that you can lead with confidence, clarity and ease; it takes time, focus and practice. I have outlined in short bursts throughout this book, some important topics to consider.

As we come to the end, what chapter do you need to read again?

_____

What is the one action item you want to be intentional about for the months ahead?

Month	Action Step I Want To Be Intentional To Practice Are:

About the Author

Sheeba Varghese is a strategic partner for your organization's talent development solutions. As a recipient of the Top Leadership Trainer Award and a Mentor to Professional Coaches, Sheeba leverages two decades of experience in her support of leaders and teams to elevate their leadership and achieve faster results through greater levels of confidence, clarity and ease. Sheeba has partnered with clients across the globe and within a broad range of industries such as law, technology, health care and financial services to name a few.

Sheeba is a Professional Certified Coach and a Certified Mentor Coach with the International Coaching Federation. She holds a dual Bachelor of Science degrees in Mathematics and Secondary Education from the University of Maryland at College Park. She is one of the Trainers of the Coach Training programs offered by Coaching Out of the Box, and continues to provide Mentor Coaching for coaches looking to become credentialed with the International Coaching Federation. Additionally, she brings her love of leadership training in the work she contributes to Hone, a virtual learning platform that provides modern leadership training. She received her Coaching certifications through the Institute for Professional Excellence in Coaching (iPEC), Sherpa Executive Coaching, InviteChange and the Life Purpose Institute (LPI). She has been a member of the Forbes Coaches Council since 2018, and was the recipient of the Top Leadership Trainer of the year with the International Association of Top Professional's award for 2020.

Sheeba's services include speaking engagements, 1:1 Executive and Leader Coaching, 360 Assessments, Leadership Development Workshops and Trainings.

She is married to her loving, patient and supportive husband, Santosh and together they have two sons, Samuel and Steven. When she is not training or coaching, she enjoys traveling, supporting families in their growth, experiencing fine dining or simply watching a great movie.

TO GET IN TOUCH:

Email: sheeba@coachsheeba.com
Phone: USA +1 650 - 741 - 6545
Website: www.coachsheeba.com

Made in the USA
Middletown, DE
01 March 2022

61998286R00046